The Babylonian Empire

Children's Middle Eastern History Books

BABY PROFESSOR

EDUCATION KIDS

Have you heard of the Hanging Gardens
of Babylons? Did you ever imagine how
impressive the gardens were? Just how rich
was the city of Babylon in ancient times?

Here are some amazing facts about the rich city of Babylon. Learn how the city rose and fell in history.

Babylon was the biggest city of the Babylonian civilization of ancient Mesopotamia. When the Sumer civilization lost power, the Babylonian Empire rose to take its place. Its center was in the south of Mesopotamia. Within the ruins of the fallen Sumerian cities, new Babylonian city-states rose up.

The city of Babylon was built in honor of the most powerful god of the Babylonians, Marduk. Babylon was the most spectacular city in the empire, and grander than any other city in the world at that time.

Two empires rose to power after the fall of the Akkadian Empire. The Babylonian Empire was in the south and the Assyrians were to its north.

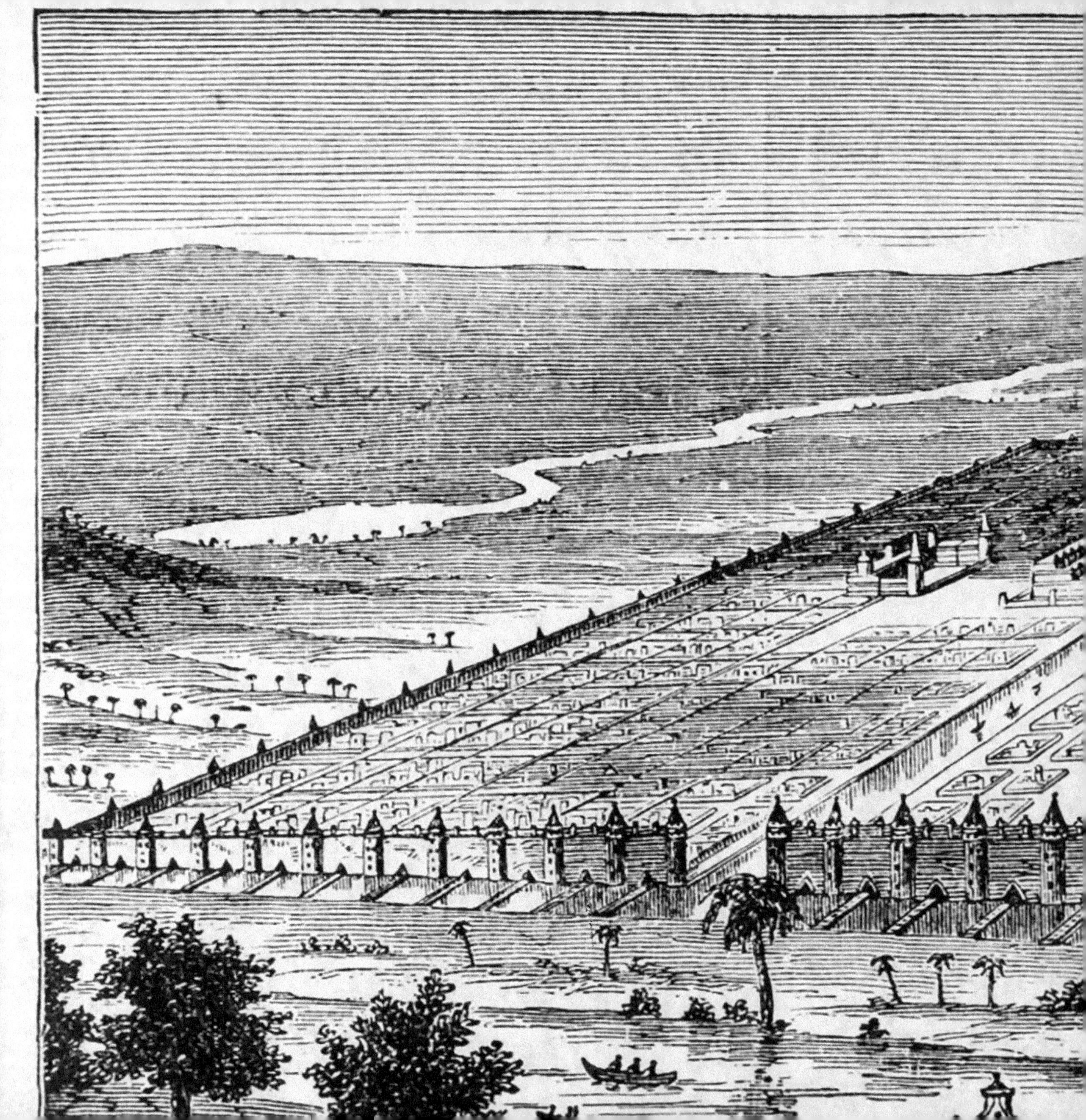

The Babylonian civilization was the first to form an empire that covered all Mesopotamia. For years, Babylon had been one of the individual city-states of Mesopotamia.

The Rise of Babylon and King Hammurabi. Babylon was taken over by the Amorites when the Akkadian empire lost power. In 1792 BC, King Hammurabi took the throne and Babylon rose in importance. King Hammurabi was powerful and conquered all the other city-states of Mesopotamia. He even conquered most of the Assyrian north.

Under the leadership of King Hammurabi, Babylon became the most powerful city in the world. The city became the center of trade. New products and ideas entered the city.

King Hammurabi became famous for the Code of Hammurabi. These were his strict laws. They are the earliest written laws that we know of in world history. The laws were written on clay tablets and on steles or tall pillars of stones, so everybody could know what was allowed and what was forbidden.

There were 282 laws in the
Code of Hammurabi. These
set guidelines for the
ways people lived, how
they could do business,
and what happened
if they committed a
crime. It talked about
trade, wages and even
the sale of slaves.

Babylon was occupied by over 200,000 people at the height ofits power. It became the largest city in the world. One the most famous attractions at the center of the city was the temple Ziggurat. It was designed like a pyramid with a flat top. It was about 300 feet tall.

The city of Babylon was really a jewel during this time as it gloried in its palaces, tall towers, magnificent gardens and impressive artwork.

Literature, astronomy
and other disciplines
flourished in the
Babylonian Empire.

The Fall of the Babylonian Empire. King Hammurabi's sons replaced him as King after his death.

However their leadership didn't succeed for they were not as good as King Hammurabi had been. The once rich city of Babylon started to lose power and to decline. The Babylonian Empire fell apart. Then the city was ruled by the Hittites.

In 1595 BC Babylon was
conquered by the Kassites,
who ruled the city for 400
years. The Kassites gave
the city its new name
as Karanduniash. After
the fall of the Kassites,
the Assyrians took over.
The Assyrians were
headed by Sennacherib.
He reigned as king from
705 to 681 BCE. His harsh
reign led to an uprising
by the Babylonians.
The city was largely
ruined in the fighting.

King Esarhaddon re-built
Babylon and brought back
glory to the ruined city.

Amazingly, Babylon rose again to power in 612 BC. The Babylonian Empire once again became so powerful that it ruled over Mesopotamia. This led to the rise of the Neo-Babylonian Empire.

Nebuchadnezzar II built the most beautiful garden in the world, the "Hanging Gardens of Babylon". It had impressive garden terraces which were 75 feet high. The gardens were crowded with beautiful flowers and plants which made the gardens one of the wonders of the world. The gardens joined the great temple of Ziggurat at the center of Babylon.

Share this book to your friends!

Visit

BABY PROFESSOR
EDUCATION KIDS

www.BabyProfessorBooks.com

to download Free Baby Professor eBooks and view
our catalog of new and exciting Children's Books